# TABLE OF CONTENTS

Screenwriter's Notebook: A Remedial Step-by-Step Guide to Finishing Your Screenplay, First Revision
By Alexander G. Valdez
Photography and Images by Alexander G. Valdez

ISBN 978-0-9848220-3-4
Ideas in this publication are registered Copyright 2012
All other material Copyright 2013 by Alexander Valdez. All rights reserved
Published by Vision Quest Entertainment Incorporated
LCCN: 2012953034

**A TEACHER'S EDITION REMEDIAL SUGGESTION GUIDE IS AVAILABLE FOR THIS BOOK. CONTACT YOUR VENDOR OR VISION QUEST ENTERTAINMENT INCORPORATED AT THE WEBSITE BELOW**

Do you have a Question, Comment, or Complaint about this product? We value your input. Help us improve our product by giving your insights at our company website.

**www.visionquestentertainmentincorporated.com**

This publication is a durable paper product.
Reduce, Reuse and Recycle.

4

# ACKNOWLEDGMENTS

I spent a semester mentor-teaching at-risk kids remedial filmmaking at Venice High School in Los Angeles Unified School District while I was getting my Master's Degree in the Fine Art of Cinema-Television Production at the University of Southern California. The class was half writing a screenplay and the second half shooting, and editing the footage. Also, the film had "graffiti" publicly made. Many of the students in my group were considered at-risk of graduation from high school. I am proud to say, all of the kids in my section graduated.

We found, as the kids were shy at the first week, and pushed to the limit by the ominous effort of post-production, they wished they had gotten more done in their first three weeks.

I have written the books in the Project Period Series to guide you in your own creating of a well-formed project through a process which will help you to write, shoot and edit your own ideas for a film, streaming media, or teleplay. The series is growing. The series includes *Our Story Begins, Screenwriter's Notebook: A Step-by-Step Guide to Finishing your Screenplay, Remedial Suggestion Guide for Screenwriter's Notebook: A Step-by-Step Guide to Finishing your Screenplay* and *A Writer's Guide to the Hero's Journey: An Introduction to the Cinema-Libre Film Movement.*

Welcome. You are about to begin a rapid process of writing, which will help you to shape the ideas in your imagination into a screenplay format. This booklet is a writing tool, an active-use reference guide, and should help you in your dramatic writing goals, as well as help you to structure documentaries and biographies, including memoirs. Feel free to write in this book. This book is your book, and the screenplay, which results from your effort, should feel like your own also. You can carry the skills you learn in this process to any endeavor you set out towards, artistic or otherwise.

Writing is a joy and something anyone can do with a little training, a healthy amount of effort and a helpful heaping of guidance. The difference in quality of writing is often affected by the goals of the writer in the creation of the work. Setting creative guidelines for yourself can help you to make a work you are proud to have completed.

Writing is sometimes predictably structural, and a well-formed structure can assist you in presenting a story with repeatable and inviting morality and ideals. This makes your story more appealing to general audiences.

If your intend to make your story into a film or video, checking and double checking your script may save you hours of effort and countless headaches in post-production. Go over the following checklist. Return to the checklist after you have made a little more progress on your script and compare the checklist to the project you have written.

# WRITER'S CHECKLIST

✓ Stories, almost always, show a lesson, which the audience can identify with and believe. Does your story have a lesson?

✓ The main tools of filmmaking involve moving your story with the use of scenes, which involve characters, setting, and action. Have you incorporated these into all of your scenes in a format similar to page 29?

✓ A story with morality and ideals you like can be interesting to an audience with similar upbringing. Have you reflected morals?

✓ Allow your audience the joy of relishing entering the world of your story. Give them enough description to let them feel immersed. In motion picture take the time to describe what is moving in the frame, and also the lighting.

✓ Stories rise in tension and eventually resolve. Does your story resolve?

✓ The rise and fall of action in a story are often described as a story's arc. Does your story rise to action?

✓ Story Arcs escalate. Does your story grow in interest?

✓ Major turning points in a story often build to each other and rely on the events earlier in the story to have the most tension and resolve. You can learn to use this build as a writer to keep your audience interested, and you yourself looking forward to finishing the next scene. Does your story have turning points?

✓ Consider the strength of upbringing of the characters versus the evolutions they make through the course of the story. Think about how well you show who they were before the story and who they have become through the story. Make a scene for each of the major intersections on the timeline.

✓ Make scenes that provide clues towards this resolution and scatter them through the story quietly as a writer. Do not depend on flashback.

✓ The reveal of new characters can greatly heighten the unanticipated nature of a story's escalation in drama. Do you use the ability of the writer to introduce characters?

✓ A Protagonist is someone who tries to accomplish something; an antagonist is someone who tries to stop a protagonist. Do you use both protagonist and antagonist? Set goals for their level of interdependence and entwining in your story. Do your secondary characters relate back to your main ones?

✓ The best stories will have the greatest struggle as the heroes get closer to the end of the story. Does your story have a conflict at the end? As you develop your story, affirm you have structure all the way to the culmination of action. Have you earned a final showdown in the arena between the opposition and the heroes? Work towards the goal.

✓ Don't forget to develop all of your scenes in your project on this notebook's scene pages, or on scene cards, which will help you in filling the scenes out more fully. Have you developed your scenes?

✓ For all forms of writing, make effort to have the right level of description. In screenplay for example, emphasize what is shown, as motion picture is showing a story.

✓ Be creative and inventive. If one of the guide questions inspires you to more than one scene, write the additional scenes as well.

✓ Develop your characters from the incidents and life-lessons that happen before incidents in the story all the way to the story completion.

✓ The conflict between the heroes and other obstacles, including their opponents, may be set from the beginning, but the growth towards climatic action at the end of the film is essential for the story to grow in interest and thrill. Does your story grow in conflict in the middle?

✓ The sand painting represents the growth and conflict of a standard three–act structure. Each place on the sandpainting lines touch each other, you would write a scene. If your story is more or less complex, adapt the scene suggestions accordingly.

✓ The feathers in the sandpainting depict new elements of story entering the sequence of progression of the actions and the goals of the characters. The overall Arc of the story should have the antagonist and protagonist lines intertwining like the feathers in the sandpainting. Do you add new elements in your story?

✓ The lighter line on the sandpainting represents a second story which has it's own ups and downs. If the story has a B story split off, why does the B story separate?

✓ Once you have written scenes, look at the scenes you have written and try to organize your scene cards in a structure similar to the sandpainting and imagine your story in terms of escalation, added interest and conflict and resolution of goals.

✓ Key nexus points of action and conflict are worth planning ahead of time, and also give your audience clues towards climax and resolution. Do you alert your audience the action is coming? Refer to the sandpainting arc and plan scenes, which foreshadow impending action and preface conflict in the arena. (See Pages 56–63)

✓ Allow for drama and showmanship at the culmination of the story at the end when the stories combine back together. In other words, allow conflict in the world of the characters and resolution of this conflict to be what brings the "B" story and the main story back together. Allow these scenes to unite characters with a combination of the heroes and the opposition. (See Pages 46–55 and 84–89)

✓ Write several scenes to fill in the blanks in your story. Anytime you feel the audience may benefit from learning something, make the effort to show them something.

✓ Have you earned another solemn look at the arena where your heroes take the time to understand their importance?

✓ Do your heroes ever take the time to refresh themselves, and the audience, on the things they have learned?

✓ Have you earned the interest from your audience to examine even further the opponents goals and upbringing? The more interesting your opponents are, the better the story.

EXPERT TIP: If your audience understands both the hero and opponent characters' goals, your story will be more well-rounded and believable.

✓ Do you have a strong enough second story in your screenplay the second story deserves development? Give the second story a solid look to see what you can add in terms of interest and also opportunity for teaching your audience about the world of your story, and also entertaining them with humor, suspense, emotional relationships, goals and possible failure.

# WRITING YOUR MAIN CHARACTER

 Considering what you have learned from the previous pages, the first step in telling a story at the most basic level is making characters which your story will revolve around. At the simple point of imagining your story, try to allow both main and secondary characters to fill your story with their own drama and goals, and also their own expertise and abilities.

What type of story do you want to tell? Most likely the characters will result from the type of movie you would like to make. Fill in the following blanks to begin your process of making the story you and your team has imagined.

✓ Design a character and place them in the narrative.

✓ Use scene cards and character cards to guide you.

On the next page, start with your main character first.

_____

EXPERT TIP: Basing characters only on people you know may limit your inventiveness. Feel free to imagine.

Your main character takes some action in your story.  What causes your character to take action?

_____

_____

_____

_____

_____

What is your main character trying to escape from or change?

_____

_____

_____

_____

What is your main character willing to risk?

_____

_____

_____

_____

How would your main character overcome obstacles?

_____

_____

_____

_____

What would make your main character shift goals?

_____

_____

_____

_____

_____

_____

_____

What does your main character struggle against?

_____

_____

_____

_____

_____

_____

_____

What will you readily show of the main character?

_____

_____

_____

_____

_____

_____

What do you reveal of the main character over time?

_____

_____

_____

_____

_____

_____

_____

What do you accentuate about the main character?

_____

_____

_____

_____

_____

Can your main character teach something? What would your character exchange for teaching?

_____

_____

_____

_____

_____

# WRITING YOUR MAIN CHARACTER
## RELATIONSHIP SECONDARY CHARACTER

Next, develop your secondary characters. For secondary characters with a relationship to the primary character, write the relationship and then the character. Know anything you need to describe to your audience, your main or secondary character may help along through similar description to another character in you movie. Your secondary characters will relate to your main characters, and may or may not be as important in the telling of your story.

Are you main characters enemies or friends? The questions on the following pages should function for anyone from lovers to buddies to enemies at war.

EXPERT TIP: Help to develop both the goals of character development and relationship depiction by bridging the gap between the characters being unique and also together by developing the relationship experience of the main and secondary characters. You may want to use additional character development cards available from www.cinema-libre.com

# MAIN and SECONDARY CHARACTERS
## Relationship Workbook Questions

First Character: _____

Male/Female

(Circle One)

College? _____

Job? _____

Interesting Thing: _____

Relationship Reasoning (why the relationship is attractive)

_____

_____

_____

_____

_____

Second Character: _____

Female/Male

(Circle One)

Job? _____

College? _____

Interesting Thing: _____

Relationship Reasoning (why the relationship is attractive)

_____

_____

_____

_____

_____

For the Relationship:

How did they meet?

_____

_____

_____

_____

_____

_____

How do they know each other?

_____

_____

_____

_____

_____

_____

What adventures have they shared?

_____

_____

_____

_____

What of the world have the two main characters seen together?

_____

_____

_____

What do they fight about?

_____

_____

_____

_____

_____

_____

What would they agree upon?

_____

_____

_____

_____

_____

_____

Why would they endure?

_____

_____

_____

_____

_____

_____

What risks do they face?

_____

_____

What is unique about them in their world?

_____

_____

_____

_____

_____

_____

Why would you give the relationship screen time, even simply to entertain your audience or add emotion?

_____

_____

_____

_____

_____

Why do these characters exist in the same world? How are they similar? How are they unique?

_____

_____

_____

_____

Use the space on the following page to develop your secondary characters.

What does your main supporting character struggle against?

_____

_____

_____

_____

What will you readily show of the supporting character?

_____

_____

_____

_____

What do you reveal of the supporting character over time?

_____

_____

_____

What do you accentuate about the supporting character?

_____

_____

_____

Can your supporting character teach something?  What would your character exchange for teaching?

_____

EXPERT TIP: Any information given in these workbook pages you would like to show in a screenplay, would require a scene to show the audience the information and would require dialogue or visual depiction in the film for the expression to your audience of the information you have written.

# WRITING YOUR OPPONENT CHARACTERS

How many opponents challenge your main character? Why have they banded together if there is more than one opponent?

_____

_____

_____

_____

_____

How are the characters fractious if there is more than one opponent?

_____

_____

_____

_____

_____

Why do these characters exist in the same world?

_____

_____

_____

_____

_____

_____

How are they similar?

_____

_____

_____

_____

_____

_____

How are they unique?

_____

_____

_____

_____

What does your opponent character struggle against?

_____

_____

_____

_____

_____

What will you readily show of the opponent character?

_____

_____

_____

_____

What do you reveal of the opponent character over time?

_____

_____

_____

_____

_____

_____

What do you accentuate about the opponent character?

_____

_____

_____

_____

_____

_____

Can your opponent character teach something?  What would
this character exchange for teaching?

_____

_____

_____

_____

_____

_____

# INCORPORATING YOUR SOCIAL GOALS

You, as a writer, may have social goal. A social goal is often important and is something you would like to change in your audience when they view your work. Your characters and their difficulties are a vessel for you to show examples of the type of stand in society you would like to make.

For the Writer:
What is something you would like to change about the world which exists in the scenes of your movie?

_____

_____

_____

_____

_____

_____

What goals do you have for the characters which show the world and changes or lack of changes?

_____

_____

_____

_____

_____

Why would your characters oppose you in your goals for change? Why would they oppose each other?

_____

_____

_____

_____

_____

_____

_____

What goals would your characters, and you, agree upon without doubt?

_____

_____

_____

_____

_____

What would you work towards having your audience learn which they would be able to carry with them?

_____

_____

_____

_____

Congratulations. You are moving increasingly close to writing your screenplay. As you write your scenes, know you will eventually place these scenes into a screenplay format. A finished feature–film screenplay is normally around 110 pages and, if your have properly written your screenplay to format, about one minute should go by in the actual movie for every page in the script. Examples of screenplay format are available online, but know you will include on each scene, no matter how short, a *Slug Line*. Slug lines give all of the information that your finished scene will be able to convey visually, for example day or night, or the physical location. Your screenplay, when finished, would looks something like this:

```
INT. CLASSROOM –DAY
Two students look at their screenwriter's
notebooks, the sun streaming into the classroom
from the windows through the blinds.  The first
Student, SARAH, fifteen and pretty has a
decorated binder.   The second student, HENRY,
has a loud shirt.   Henry has chosen to sit
next to Sarah.

                    SARAH
        I think I understand this example.

                    HENRY
        We should begin writing.

                    SARAH
            I agree.


The students both get to work.  Henry stands to
sharpen his pencil, and returns to sit next to
Sarah, who has begun working.  Their pencils
sharpened and pens at the ready.

They continue to progress until Sarah looks at
Henry and smiles.  The smile is returned.
```

As you see on the previous page, the characters' names are in capital letters the very first time in the screenplay the characters are introduced. Sluglines (The INT. CLASSROOM - DAY) tell you exactly where and when in lighting the scene is and will be followed by a setting description. INT is the abbreviation for interior, EXT is the abbreviation of exterior. For something like a car where you are in both a little, you would use the abbreviation INT./EXT. The Characters names in the dialogue are in capital letters, the dialogue is centered. Spaces in action are normally spaced with a full line of space between, as also noted on the previous page. You may end up using more space, but you will have a way to guess how long your movie will be. On normal 8.5 by 11-inch paper, each page will be about one minute long in your movie.

---

EXPERT TIP: Notice with the example on the previous page, in your filmmaking, the smile between the students gives you an opportunity in editing if you have the footage. The edit of the example on the previous page may have been more familiar and interesting if at the description break (the space between the blocks of description, similar to paragraphs) your director and cinematographer (camera person) choose to at least have close-up coverage of the two students' faces. Almost always these breaks in the blocks of description signal to your production team a change in the type of coverage, or shot design.

You can easily use these close-ups in your editing as the physical space between the two students is defined to the audience in the beginning of the scene and we have not left the physical space in our editing. Most audience members would like to see up close the characters' feelings and relationship. Try the example in your class environment to experiment with the camera and editing equipment and see what you would choose in your edit.

---

# TWELVE STORY QUESTION PICTOGRAPHS FOR THE WRITER

As you move forward with your writing, consider the following twelve questions:

1. Do you have characters?
2. Do your characters have goals?
3. Are your characters ever trapped?
4. Are your characters well enough developed?
5. What can your characters teach someone?  What do they exchange?
6. What can your characters accomplish?
7. Why?
8. What have they learned which can help?
9. Are your characters ever physical?
10. Is their goal absolute?
11. What sacrifice would they face?
12. What goes wrong?  How do they progress?

---

EXPERT TIP: If you are self-producing, at the point you feel comfortable with your screenplay, you will be ready for a table read with your actors.  A table read has all of the involved performers get together to hear the script read out loud.  The very next step is to begin filming.  Make sure to have the right permissions in place as you begin to record your images.

---

## Do you have characters?

Writers often start screenplays by imagining characters they find interesting. By using diverse characters you will be able to explore complex concepts in simple ways.

Introducing characters you are proud of in a story is a fun and interesting thing as a writer to get to do. Imaginative characters are fun for your audience and fun for you to get to explore. Diverse characters that represent distinct and pure traits are examples of archetypes. Archetypes drive mythology.

EXPERT TIP: Characters who learn the rules they play by in your story allow you to share the rules with the audience.

### Do your characters have goals?

All characters have conflict. Often their conflicts arise from goals. The type of goals will determine where your character chooses to exist and towards what they choose to endeavor. As you tell your story, try to solve as many dilemmas as you can with the decision making and resulting action appearing to come from your characters. This creates character driven drama.

EXPERT TIP: Your story structure is only as interesting as your characters' goals.

## Are your characters ever trapped?

Through the course of their story, your characters may become trapped, even for a little while. The shorter the story, the more they may fixate on simply being free. Compare their being trapped to the goals you set for them. Are the goals you set for them and their entrapment antithetical? The types of entrapment your characters can endure can be as complex as you can imagine. Being trapped can be both physical and conceptual. The best course of storytelling may involve elements of their world closing in around them and slowly eliminating their choices. They may respond boldly.

As you begin to imagine the characters in a physical environment, there may be benefit to imagining them locked in a building or even an elevator simply to begin to explore their problem solving capability and their uniqueness. There may be more enrichment to imagining them locked into a deal from which they cannot escape. They may have a legal quandary, they may have agreed to a ruthless bargain.

---

EXPERT TIP: The shorter the film or scene exchange of the characters, the more valuable a "ticking clock" or time limit is to the suspense and drama of your story.

---

**Are your characters well enough developed?**

Characters should have a rich background, even if much of the information you devote to their story goes beyond what feels directly pertinent. Remember, in a medium like motion picture you are showing a story and you may be amazed at how much information you can convey to the audience without much devotion of time in your storytelling by incorporating visual elements to fill in the life of the characters.

EXPERT TIP: Audiences get to know your characters when the characters discuss things in an interesting way, even if the discussion is well beyond the plot.

**What can your characters teach someone?  What do they exchange?**

Characters who are teachers are often very interesting to explore. Showing the gain of knowledge your characters endure will most likely improve your project. The benefit is two-fold. You can improve your project and also inform your audience. Your audience may take a beautiful selfish interest in your work simply because of what you have allowed them to learn and know.

Ask yourself, do your teacher characters teach what they teach for pay? Do they share goals with the heroes to the point they give knowledge? How far can you take your characters with what you, yourself, know? Are your principal characters the teachers or do you introduce a new character to teach them? Do you go backwards in the story you have presented in order to establish these characters? Are they legendary or just the guys next door? How sacred is their knowledge?

---

EXPERT TIP: Keep what your teacher characters give as knowledge realistic, at least to what you can show your audience with your level of special effects and traditional filmmaking techniques.

---

### What can your characters accomplish?

Characters can do things a normal human cannot. Have you given your characters enough interesting characteristics about them to ensure they are extraordinary and cinematically worthy? Do they have enough opportunity in your story to show their skills? Have you begun to explore, with your audience observing, why in your story they are suited to be the hero? Make them extraordinary and distinct.

EXPERT TIP: Consider having your characters challenged with something more difficult than they have ever faced before.

## Why?

Why are certain elements in your story? Why have you or your characters made the decisions presented in your story? Explore new elements. If you have spent a month on each of these twelve concepts diligently, by now you should have enough of your story in place to be able to pour back over your writing and question everything you have written in both decision making and believability.

Holding nothing of your fiction as protected, allow yourself to critique decisions both you and your characters hold dear. Challenge everything.

---

EXPERT TIP: If you let go of what you hold most dear in your story to improve your storytelling, once the story is at a certain level of development, those elements may trickle back in later.

---

### What have they learned which can help?

Consider having your characters learn something in the course of their adventure. Again, examine teacher characters. Consider your heroes or their opponents discovering something of great importance. If solutions were simple, they wouldn't be worth the story you intend to tell. What have your characters undergone to be ready? How much of this do you share? Teaching is sometimes parable by example; do your characters learn something by simply watching someone or hearing a story? What do they gain?

EXPERT TIP: Reiterating knowledge later in your project may help your audience, especially if you intend to educate children.

**Are your characters ever physical?**

The greatest stories almost always have a physical element. What can your characters accomplish in the world in which they exist? Are they physically unique? Even if they do not have a physical element for their job, are they physically active? Do the characters play any sports with each other? Could a dialogue scene be done on a racquetball court for example? Do your romantic characters dance? Can the children play baseball? Are there elements of them interacting with animals? Do they interact with each other through their world, such as holding the door open for each other? Are they strong? Do they suffer cruelty?

EXPERT TIP: Filming scenes with action may increase the amount of footage you need, including complexity of angles. Plan accordingly.

### Is their goal absolute?

Changes in the game plan for your characters allow you to show their drive and inventiveness. The best plan for your characters is often the plan they concoct as the audience observes. Your characters may be able to overcome many of their difficulties by streamlining their objectives. Both protagonist and antagonist have goals. Are their goals absolute? What would make them change their goals?

EXPERT TIP: Characters with adjustable prejudice or bias can adapt to new goals. Good guys can often adapt.

### What sacrifice would they face?

Nothing great comes without sacrifice. This is no less true in life than in the journey of your characters. What do your characters forfeit or relinquish? What do they forgo? Is part of their sacrifice based on what they need to endure?

Ultimately, your heroes will have to give something up to attain their goal. Will they give up their purity? Will they give up something they put in effort towards other than the main goal? Will they lose their family connections or friendships? Will they risk them?

---

EXPERT TIP: Audiences feel empathy if your characters must give away something they hold dear.

---

### What goes wrong?  How do they progress?

Challenge your characters to the point you feel their failure may be imminent and their success is never guaranteed.  We want to see them triumph over insurmountable odds and overcome inconceivable obstacles.  The difficulties the characters triumph over benefit the genuineness, in their world, of the resolve (see pages 106–112).  Genuineness helps people to believe your story.  Keep your story within the bounds of what people feel and know, or what you as a filmmaker can show, but keep your characters impressive.

EXPERT TIP: Audiences enjoy seeing characters solve problems.

# THE NEXT STEP

The next part of the workbook is the main part of the writing. You will have to have had characters to have gotten this far, but the scenes are the bulk of your planning of your project. Scenes will determine your production locations and who and what you will need on your production days.

Consider this upcoming process step by step. As you move onto the next scene suggestion place your ideas onto a new scene page. Unless you are very inspired, you will not likely fill in all of these gaps without some time to rest and think in between scenes. Go over these following scene pages often, and refer back to the questions any time you get stuck. With concept after concept, be comfortable to stay as close as possible to initial inspiration as you can. You will have a chance to polish these when you move to the next stage and write your screenplay.

EXPERT TIP: While using this notebook, if at first an idea doesn't come to you for a certain space on the scene page, move onto the next scene suggestion and continue with your first impressions. Don't judge your ideas. Simply fill in the open boxes on the scene cards or move onto the next concept. Later, return to the vacant boxes on the Scene Development Cards and give them sincere meditation. Move your scenes around in your story's chronology to best improve your results in the overall sequence of scenes in the story's arc. Add characters if necessary. If you feel a scene you create needs prompting, write a scene for earlier in your chronology, which sets the current scene into your story well.

# THE EIGHT ELEMENTS OF STORY

The Eight Elements of Story represent aspects essential for the most interesting and most engaging depiction of the hero or heroine. Read the writings on each topic in this publication and compare them to the story you have structured. The ideas are applicable to novels, novellas, short stories, epic poems and all television scripts and films including documentary films and narrative films. For documentary mediums, you may choose to exemplify these ideals in editing and image selection. How well has your story incorporated all of these elements?

### The Eight Elements of Story In Brief:

THE HERO is who the story revolves around.

THE ARENA is where the hero is proven.

THE SPECTACLE is how and when the hero is proven.

THE GOALS are what of the hero is proven.

THE OPPOSITION is who the heroes are proven against.

THE GAIN is what the hero gets.

THE BENEFIT is what the hero gives.

THE RESOLVE is what remains which is lasting.

As you are learning how to incorporate these eight elements into your screenplay, write one scene for each of the following scene suggestions on the page immediately after the scene suggestion.

When you combine them into your screenplay, know you can move the scenes around in relationship to each other. If you are writing for a short film, you may pick and choose what scenes to develop. If you are using separate scene cards, place your scene cards in the order you think creates the best arcing sequence for the best story.

EXPERT TIP: Jot your ideas with pencil in the areas provided and fill in the scene cards when you and any collaborators agree on your goals.

## Developing who the story revolves around.

Your heroes are your champions around whom the story revolves. They are often brave and even if they are not normally courageous, they are at least courageous enough to accomplish a goal. Consider the following types of concepts as you imagine your characters: How does your character grow? What does your character learn to know? What types of actions will your character enact which may have repercussions or a penalty?

The type of hero or heroine in your story determines the type of story told. If your hero or heroine is a warrior, he or she will most likely solve resistance with fighting. If your hero or heroine is intelligent, he or she will most likely solve dilemmas with thought. If your hero or heroine is cunning, he or she will most likely solve quandary with guile. If your hero or heroine is wise, he or she will most likely solve problems with wisdom. Your heroes have some skill or ability that sets them apart. They have learned these skills, or know them innately. They will summon these skills from within themselves or gain them through the teachings of others. They will practice and they will learn, and the audience will love them for their adventure.

## CONSIDER THE FOLLOWING SCENE SUGGESTION:

On the next page, write a scene in which your hero character physically does something unique to establish them as different than the other characters in their world.

Scene Location Description: Interior/Exterior:

Day/Night/Sunrise/Sunset/Magic Hour

(Circle One)

Characters involved:

Scene opens with:

Basic Action:

What of the characters is revealed in the scene?

What does the scene advance about the story?

What causes your character to take action?

Notes:

## CONSIDER THE FOLLOWING SCENE SUGGESTION:

On the next page, write a scene in which your hero relays something which happened to them in their childhood.

EXPERT TIP: Consider the objects your characters choose to carry with them. What do they consider valuable?

Scene Location Description: Interior/Exterior:

Day/Night/Sunrise/Sunset/Magic Hour

(Circle One)

Characters involved:

Scene opens with:

Basic Action:

What of the characters is revealed in the scene?

What does the scene advance about the story?

What causes your character to take action?

Notes:

## CONSIDER THE FOLLOWING SCENE SUGGESTION:

On the next page, write a scene where one of your main characters expresses something they would like to learn or accomplish.

_____

_____

_____

_____

_____

_____

Scene Location Description: Interior/Exterior: _____

Day/Night/Sunrise/Sunset/Magic Hour

(Circle One)

Characters involved: _____

Scene opens with: _____

Basic Action: _____

What of the characters is revealed in the scene? _____

What does the scene advance about the story? _____

What causes your character to take action? _____

Notes: _____

## CONSIDER THE FOLLOWING SCENE SUGGESTION:

On the next page, write a scene that suggests your character lacks maturity and is not yet up to the challenges.

Scene Location Description: Interior/Exterior:

Day/Night/Sunrise/Sunset/Magic Hour

(Circle One)

Characters involved:

Scene opens with:

Basic Action:

What of the characters is revealed in the scene?

What does the scene advance about the story?

What causes your character to take action?

Notes:

## CONSIDER THE FOLLOWING SCENE SUGGESTION:

On the next page, write a scene where your hero characters endeavor to improve themselves.

Scene Location Description: Interior/Exterior:

_____
Day/Night/Sunrise/Sunset/Magic Hour
_____
(Circle One)

Characters involved:
_____
_____

Scene opens with:
_____
_____
_____

Basic Action:
_____
_____
_____

What of the characters is revealed in the scene?
_____
_____

What does the scene advance about the story?
_____
_____

What causes your character to take action?
_____
_____
_____

Notes:
_____
_____
_____
_____
_____

## Developing where the hero is proven.

If your heroes endeavor and succeed or fail, they will be proven and the arena is the proving ground of champions. The arena will most likely be suited to the type of hero or heroine you have written. If they barter for a living, they may have the arena of a stock or futures floor or a boardroom, if they fight for a living they may find themselves in a boxing ring. If they are gladiators, they may find themselves in the coliseum. If they are lawyers they may find themselves in a courtroom. There is both a location and a time in the arena, and screenplay format will allow every scene, even short scenes while intercutting, to define this location and time for each scene so the production crew know where to shoot and the producers know where to ready the location of the shooting set and the legal for the productions such as permission to shoot there.

In the story, the Arena gives them a setting and most likely also a set of rules. The most interesting long form stories will also show your characters in venues other than their main arena.

EXPERT TIP: When imaging the arena, consider if you were making your movie a puppet show, what would you have to build for the stage?

## CONSIDER THE FOLLOWING SCENE SUGGESTION:

On the next page, write a scene where the arena proving grounds are displayed. While entertaining your audience, teach them the rules of the playing field where your hero characters will be tested.

Scene Location Description: Interior/Exterior: _____

Day/Night/Sunrise/Sunset/Magic Hour
_____

(Circle One)

Characters involved: _____
_____

Scene opens with: _____
_____
_____

Basic Action: _____
_____
_____
_____

What of the characters is revealed in the scene? _____

What does the scene advance about the story? _____

What causes your character to take action? _____
_____
_____

Notes: _____
_____
_____
_____
_____

## CONSIDER THE FOLLOWING SCENE SUGGESTION:

On the next page, write a scene in which your characters have an initial showing of capability in the arena. Are they bested? Do they show talent or skill?

Scene Location Description: Interior/Exterior: _____

Day/Night/Sunrise/Sunset/Magic Hour

(Circle One)

Characters involved: _____

Scene opens with: _____

_____

_____

Basic Action: _____

_____

_____

What of the characters is revealed in the scene? _____

What does the scene advance about the story? _____

What causes your character to take action? _____

_____

Notes: _____

_____

_____

_____

_____

## CONSIDER THE FOLLOWING SCENE SUGGESTION:

On the next page, write a scene where the determination of the hero characters is tested. Allow them to change or show determination.

EXPERT TIP: Remember, these scenes can be in a different order in your screenplay.

Scene Location Description: Interior/Exterior:

_____

Day/Night/Sunrise/Sunset/Magic Hour

_____

(Circle One)

Characters involved:

_____

_____

Scene opens with:

_____

_____

_____

Basic Action:

_____

_____

_____

_____

What of the characters is revealed in the scene?

_____

_____

What does the scene advance about the story?

_____

_____

What causes your character to take action?

_____

_____

_____

Notes:

_____

_____

_____

_____

_____

## CONSIDER THE FOLLOWING SCENE SUGGESTION:

On the next page, write a scene where the hero spends time on the proving ground away from competition. Allow them the physical space with a lessened level of proving and threat.

Scene Location Description: Interior/Exterior:

_____

Day/Night/Sunrise/Sunset/Magic Hour

(Circle One)

Characters involved:

_____

Scene opens with:

_____

_____

Basic Action:

_____

_____

_____

What of the characters is revealed in the scene?

_____

What does the scene advance about the story?

_____

What causes your character to take action?

_____

_____

Notes:

_____

_____

_____

_____

### Developing how and when the hero is proven.

The agitation, commotion and excitement in the arena often have a time and place to occur such as trading is open, the fight is on or the jury is assembled. The type of exchange the heroes endure is often public and often with physical action, sensational.

Just as the real world audience observes the heroes, so too does the average person in their world. As a writer embellish the conflict and details of risk for the heroes and let your audience relish in the amount of poetic description and sensational exchange the spectacle can bring. In film, visually celebrate the heroes, their opponents, and even their observers. You have taken the time and effort to get your audience there and you may now take the opportunity to thrill them.

In literature, any character singled out is special, so even writing of a face in the crowd makes them different. Instead of considering the average person unimportant, flesh them well enough to at least make them an archetype and allow them to be the witnesses for the heroes' spectacle. This maximizes the vicarious association with the spectacle of the heroes' challenge, and also the granting of the audience freely given action and thrill as the heroes' observer.

### CONSIDER THE FOLLOWING SCENE SUGGESTION:

On the next page, write a scene in which characters other than your heroes create and say openly the rules for evaluating the success of your characters.

Scene Location Description: Interior/Exterior:

_____

Day/Night/Sunrise/Sunset/Magic Hour

(Circle One)

Characters involved:

_____

Scene opens with:

_____

_____

_____

Basic Action:

_____

_____

_____

What of the characters is revealed in the scene?

_____

What does the scene advance about the story?

_____

What causes your character to take action?

_____

_____

Notes:

_____

_____

_____

_____

## CONSIDER THE FOLLOWING SCENE SUGGESTION:

On the next page, write a scene in which other characters are going to take interest in your main hero characters and their journey.

Scene Location Description: Interior/Exterior:

_____

Day/Night/Sunrise/Sunset/Magic Hour

(Circle One)

Characters involved:

_____

Scene opens with:

_____

_____

Basic Action:

_____

_____

What of the characters is revealed in the scene?

_____

What does the scene advance about the story?

_____

What causes your character to take action?

_____

_____

Notes:

_____

_____

_____

_____

## CONSIDER THE FOLLOWING SCENE SUGGESTION:

On the next page, write a scene where the stakes in the arena increase.

Scene Location Description: Interior/Exterior:

_____

Day/Night/Sunrise/Sunset/Magic Hour

(Circle One)

Characters involved:

_____

Scene opens with:

_____

_____

Basic Action:

_____

_____

_____

What of the characters is revealed in the scene?

_____

What does the scene advance about the story?

_____

What causes your character to take action?

_____

_____

Notes:

_____

_____

_____

_____

## CONSIDER THE FOLLOWING SCENE SUGGESTION:

On the next page, write a scene where your characters are encouraged by other characters in the story.

Scene Location Description: Interior/Exterior:

_____

Day/Night/Sunrise/Sunset/Magic Hour

(Circle One)

Characters involved:

_____

Scene opens with:

_____

_____

Basic Action:

_____

_____

What of the characters is revealed in the scene?

_____

What does the scene advance about the story?

_____

What causes your character to take action?

_____

_____

Notes:

_____

_____

_____

_____

## CONSIDER THE FOLLOWING SCENE SUGGESTION:

On the next page, write a scene where someone other than your heroes wins or loses something, other than the largest goal.

Scene Location Description: Interior/Exterior:

_____

Day/Night/Sunrise/Sunset/Magic Hour

(Circle One)

Characters involved:

_____

Scene opens with:

_____

_____

Basic Action:

_____

_____

_____

What of the characters is revealed in the scene?

_____

What does the scene advance about the story?

_____

What causes your character to take action?

_____

_____

Notes:

_____

_____

_____

_____

## CONSIDER THE FOLLOWING SCENE SUGGESTION:

On the next page, write a scene where a character younger than your hero character sets an intention to emulate the hero in success.

---

_____

_____

_____

_____

_____

_____

Scene Location Description: Interior/Exterior:

_____

Day/Night/Sunrise/Sunset/Magic Hour

(Circle One)

Characters involved:

_____

Scene opens with:

_____

_____

Basic Action:

_____

_____

_____

What of the characters is revealed in the scene?

_____

What does the scene advance about the story?

_____

What causes your character to take action?

_____

_____

Notes:

_____

_____

_____

_____

# WRITING THE GOALS

Developing what of the hero is proven.

The heroes set goals both for themselves and for their adventure. The goals define the type of hero or heroine your character will be and, as mentioned before, the type of hero or heroine they are determines the story. If your audience emotes with the characters as they set their goals, they will be empathetic with them all the way to the end of the story and beyond. The heroes will resonate in your audiences' emotions and the opponents will be well rounded and well received.

Goals can be physical, financial, emotional, social, intimate, personal, shared by a group or any other adjective you can think of to allow your characters the best expression of what they would like to achieve. The greater the goal, the greater the hero or heroine.

## CONSIDER THE FOLLOWING SCENE SUGGESTION:

On the next page, write a scene where your characters express determination towards goals in which they establish for themselves what success will be and what they are willing to risk.

_____

_____

_____

_____

_____

Scene Location Description: Interior/Exterior:

_____

Day/Night/Sunrise/Sunset/Magic Hour

(Circle One)

Characters involved:

_____

Scene opens with:

_____

_____

Basic Action:

_____

_____

_____

What of the characters is revealed in the scene?

_____

What does the scene advance about the story?

_____

What causes your character to take action?

_____

_____

Notes:

_____

_____

_____

_____

## CONSIDER THE FOLLOWING SCENE SUGGESTION:

On the next page, write a scene where your heroes are motivated by a partial success.

Scene Location Description: Interior/Exterior:

Day/Night/Sunrise/Sunset/Magic Hour

(Circle One)

Characters involved:

Scene opens with:

Basic Action:

What of the characters is revealed in the scene?

What does the scene advance about the story?

What causes your character to take action?

Notes:

## CONSIDER THE FOLLOWING SCENE SUGGESTION:

On the next page, write a scene where your hero does something selfish.

Scene Location Description: Interior/Exterior:

_____

Day/Night/Sunrise/Sunset/Magic Hour

(Circle One)

Characters involved:

_____

Scene opens with:

_____

_____

Basic Action:

_____

_____

_____

What of the characters is revealed in the scene?

_____

What does the scene advance about the story?

_____

What causes your character to take action?

_____

_____

Notes:

_____

_____

_____

_____

## CONSIDER THE FOLLOWING SCENE SUGGESTION:

On the next page, write a scene where a time limit is place on the characters in some way, preferably towards the largest goal.

Scene Location Description: Interior/Exterior:

_____

Day/Night/Sunrise/Sunset/Magic Hour

(Circle One)

Characters involved:

_____

Scene opens with:

_____

_____

Basic Action:

_____

_____

_____

What of the characters is revealed in the scene?

_____

What does the scene advance about the story?

_____

What causes your character to take action?

_____

_____

Notes:

_____

_____

_____

_____

# WRITING THE OPPOSITION

Developing who the heroes are proven against.

The characters at odds with the heroes are as important as the goals. They are the antagonists or protagonists depending on your structure. Generally, a protagonist tries to accomplish a goal and an antagonist tries to stop a goal. If described as enemies, they are challenged both by their enemy and by their world. The better-formed heroes will have external and also internal struggles. They may need to face and defeat their own demons. To be successful, they and the opponent characters may need to find or originate a new system of organization or control. These challenges and the heroes' rise against them substantiate the opposition. A substantial opponent makes for an interesting challenge.

Consider the questions you asked of your hero characters for the opposition as well. What does the opposition learn? How does the opposition grow? What does the opposition enact which may have repercussions or penalty?

## CONSIDER THE FOLLOWING SCENE SUGGESTION:

On the next page, write a scene in which the opponent characters choose now as the moment to act. If this is the first time your audience sees the opposition, begin at an event already in action for a point of origin.

Scene Location Description: Interior/Exterior:

_____

Day/Night/Sunrise/Sunset/Magic Hour

(Circle One)

Characters involved:

_____

Scene opens with:

_____

_____

Basic Action:

_____

_____

_____

What of the characters is revealed in the scene?

_____

What does the scene advance about the story?

_____

What causes your character to take action?

_____

_____

Notes:

_____

_____

_____

_____

## CONSIDER THE FOLLOWING SCENE SUGGESTION:

On the next page, write a scene where the opposition characters strike a deal with other characters.

_____

_____

_____

_____

_____

Scene Location Description: Interior/Exterior:

_____

Day/Night/Sunrise/Sunset/Magic Hour

(Circle One)

Characters involved:

_____

Scene opens with:

_____

_____

Basic Action:

_____

_____

_____

What of the characters is revealed in the scene?

_____

What does the scene advance about the story?

_____

What causes your character to take action?

_____

_____

Notes:

_____

_____

_____

_____

## CONSIDER THE FOLLOWING SCENE SUGGESTION:

On the next page, write a scene where the opponent characters show their level of preparation.

Scene Location Description: Interior/Exterior:

_____

Day/Night/Sunrise/Sunset/Magic Hour

(Circle One)

Characters involved:

_____

Scene opens with:

_____

_____

_____

Basic Action:

_____

_____

_____

What of the characters is revealed in the scene?

_____

What does the scene advance about the story?

_____

What causes your character to take action?

_____

_____

Notes:

_____

_____

_____

_____

Developing what the hero gets.

Most stories in which the character is proven a hero or heroine, the audience is allowed to see the character at the beginning of the story would not have been able to have triumphed against the challenges they face at the end of the story, unless they grew in study, skill, knowledge or sensitivity. The characters at the end of the story are better informed and more ready than they were at the beginning. They have learned and grown more practiced and educated. Through the course of their adventure, the skills of both the heroes and their opponents improve and their readiness is mustered. This affirms the gain and the heroes may prove themselves capable if they had endeavored to this type of gain.

Also, more often than not, your hero characters will be richer for the experience in their wealth, social affluence, fame or relationships. What you show your characters gaining in your story will make them more believable and more understandable to the audience. If you are inspired to spend more of your audience's time on these concepts, contemplate using additional scene cards from www.cinema-libre.com.

## CONSIDER THE FOLLOWING SCENE SUGGESTION:

On the next page, write a scene where your characters describe what wealth is to them. Are they covetous? Is a similar scene worth writing for the opponent characters?

_____

_____

_____

_____

_____

Scene Location Description: Interior/Exterior:

_____

Day/Night/Sunrise/Sunset/Magic Hour

(Circle One)

Characters involved:

_____

Scene opens with:

_____

_____

Basic Action:

_____

_____

_____

What of the characters is revealed in the scene?

_____

What does the scene advance about the story?

_____

What causes your character to take action?

_____

_____

Notes:

_____

_____

_____

_____

## CONSIDER THE FOLLOWING SCENE SUGGESTION:

Why haven't your characters solved these problems earlier in chronology? On the next page, write a scene that shows what the characters have to learn in order to be successful.

Scene Location Description: Interior/Exterior:

_____

Day/Night/Sunrise/Sunset/Magic Hour

(Circle One)

Characters involved:

_____

Scene opens with:

_____

_____

Basic Action:

_____

_____

_____

What of the characters is revealed in the scene?

_____

What does the scene advance about the story?

_____

What causes your character to take action?

_____

_____

Notes:

_____

_____

_____

_____

## CONSIDER THE FOLLOWING SCENE SUGGESTION:

On the next page, write a scene where one of your main characters expresses something they would like to learn or accomplish.

Scene Location Description: Interior/Exterior:

_____

Day/Night/Sunrise/Sunset/Magic Hour

(Circle One)

Characters involved:

_____

Scene opens with:

_____

_____

Basic Action:

_____

_____

_____

What of the characters is revealed in the scene?

_____

What does the scene advance about the story?

_____

What causes your character to take action?

_____

_____

Notes:

_____

_____

_____

_____

## CONSIDER THE FOLLOWING SCENE SUGGESTION:

Considering the spectacle, what will your characters accomplishing the goals bring about for them? Do they have clear objectives? On the next page, write a scene that establishes for your audience the benefit for your characters of succeeding in their goals.

Scene Location Description: Interior/Exterior:

_____

Day/Night/Sunrise/Sunset/Magic Hour
_____

(Circle One)

Characters involved:

_____

Scene opens with:

_____

_____

_____

Basic Action:

_____

_____

_____

What of the characters is revealed in the scene?

_____

What does the scene advance about the story?

_____

What causes your character to take action?

_____

_____

Notes:

_____

_____

_____

_____

## CONSIDER THE FOLLOWING SCENE SUGGESTION:

On the next page, write a scene where a new character is able to teach something to your heroes or at least spur them to their goal.

EXPERT TIP: Refer back to your script often as you edit and refine, and know you should not be afraid to move your scenes around in relationship to each other in order to give your story the most interesting arc and resolve.

Scene Location Description: Interior/Exterior:

_____

Day/Night/Sunrise/Sunset/Magic Hour

(Circle One)

Characters involved:

_____

Scene opens with:

_____

_____

_____

Basic Action:

_____

_____

_____

What of the characters is revealed in the scene?

_____

What does the scene advance about the story?

_____

What causes your character to take action?

_____

_____

Notes:

_____

_____

_____

_____

## CONSIDER THE FOLLOWING SCENE SUGGESTION:

On the next page, write a scene where the opponent characters increase their resolve.

Scene Location Description: Interior/Exterior:

_____

Day/Night/Sunrise/Sunset/Magic Hour

(Circle One)

Characters involved:

_____

Scene opens with:

_____

_____

Basic Action:

_____

_____

_____

What of the characters is revealed in the scene?

_____

What does the scene advance about the story?

_____

What causes your character to take action?

_____

_____

Notes:

_____

_____

_____

_____

## CONSIDER THE FOLLOWING SCENE SUGGESTION:

On the next page, write a scene where your hero characters are given something physically.

Scene Location Description: Interior/Exterior:

_____

Day/Night/Sunrise/Sunset/Magic Hour

(Circle One)

Characters involved:

_____

Scene opens with:

_____

_____

Basic Action:

_____

_____

_____

What of the characters is revealed in the scene?

_____

What does the scene advance about the story?

_____

What causes your character to take action?

_____

_____

Notes:

_____

_____

_____

_____

## CONSIDER THE FOLLOWING SCENE SUGGESTION:

On the next page, write a turning point scene in which your main character demonstrates they are now capable of the ultimate challenge they face. A turning point scene is often so important to the story, the course of action is affected by the change.

Scene Location Description: Interior/Exterior:

_____

Day/Night/Sunrise/Sunset/Magic Hour

(Circle One)

Characters involved:

_____

Scene opens with:

_____

_____

Basic Action:

_____

_____

_____

What of the characters is revealed in the scene?

_____

What does the scene advance about the story?

_____

What causes your character to take action?

_____

_____

Notes:

_____

_____

_____

_____

Developing what the hero gives.

Even beyond the gain, there is something larger than the heroes, left altered from the adventure that improves the universal whole. If the Gain is what the heroes gain, the Benefit is what the heroes give. In other words, the positive effect from their heroic effort and adventure leaves the world of the characters changed for the best or at least for the better.

Traditionally, characters other than just the heroes will have an improved existence for the heroes' journey and triumph. The fulfillment of this benefit for the larger, more permanent good is worth attaining. In such a story their whole community should win and they, as a result, are worth remembering.

The heroes being worth remembering is often what makes their story worth telling, and the moral of their story worth holding. This worthiness and moral demonstrates the benefit.

## CONSIDER THE FOLLOWING SCENE SUGGESTION:

On the next page, write a scene where an increasing number of characters increase advantage from the success of the heroes.

Scene Location Description: Interior/Exterior:

_____

Day/Night/Sunrise/Sunset/Magic Hour

(Circle One)

Characters involved:

_____

Scene opens with:

_____

_____

Basic Action:

_____

_____

_____

What of the characters is revealed in the scene?

_____

What does the scene advance about the story?

_____

What causes your character to take action?

_____

_____

Notes:

_____

_____

_____

_____

## CONSIDER THE FOLLOWING SCENE SUGGESTION:

On the next page, write a scene where one or more characters expresses to another a benefit for their world they would like to bring about.

_____

_____

_____

_____

_____

_____

Scene Location Description: Interior/Exterior:

_____

Day/Night/Sunrise/Sunset/Magic Hour

(Circle One)

Characters involved:

_____

Scene opens with:

_____

_____

_____

Basic Action:

_____

_____

_____

What of the characters is revealed in the scene?

_____

What does the scene advance about the story?

_____

What causes your character to take action?

_____

_____

Notes:

_____

_____

_____

_____

## CONSIDER THE FOLLOWING SCENE SUGGESTION:

Allow a scene where an authority character other than your heroes is able to relay to them the benefits of their actions. The authority may be more or less important than the heroes in their world. Write the scene on the next page.

Scene Location Description: Interior/Exterior:

Day/Night/Sunrise/Sunset/Magic Hour

(Circle One)

Characters involved:

Scene opens with:

Basic Action:

What of the characters is revealed in the scene?

What does the scene advance about the story?

What causes your character to take action?

Notes:

## CONSIDER THE FOLLOWING SCENE SUGGESTION:

On the next page, write a scene showing your characters are not yet up to the challenges they need to face in the events of their story due to something beyond their control. What combination of luck, skill, or determination carries them through?

Scene Location Description: Interior/Exterior: _____

_____

Day/Night/Sunrise/Sunset/Magic Hour

(Circle One)

Characters involved: _____

_____

Scene opens with: _____

_____

_____

Basic Action: _____

_____

_____

What of the characters is revealed in the scene? _____

_____

What does the scene advance about the story? _____

_____

What causes your character to take action? _____

_____

_____

Notes: _____

_____

_____

_____

_____

# WRITING THE RESOLVE

## Developing what remains which is lasting.

Eventually, the adventure of every hero comes to a close. The resolve is proven by what the people other than your heroes are willing to do themselves with what the heroes have taught them and exemplified. In a return to normalcy, the average person must carry forward what the heroes and champions have left behind. The ongoing effort by the average person, the heroes and society demonstrates their resoluteness. The more significant the resolve, the more important the benefit of the venture. Consider as a storyteller, how much time and emphasis would you spend on closure of such importance? Can your characters be thanked at least with a promise from the community? Will a younger warrior pick up a sword? Does stock trading simply open for another day? Does a vendor carry a new product? Does a custodian turn off the lights in the arena?

Consider your storytelling medium. Can a physical example like a ride into a sunset do more than a speech? If you are showing or describing things in a way which is hyper–real can an effect like a time lapse advance your story; for example does a flower spring?

Characters other than your principal characters will often give or teach your hero characters something. How do they comment on the resolve? Do they express approval in whole or part? Consider your arena, your observers and your heroes and allow them each their own resolve.

## CONSIDER THE FOLLOWING SCENE SUGGESTION:

On the next page, write a scene where your hero characters restate their goals and add determination.

Scene Location Description: Interior/Exterior:

_____

Day/Night/Sunrise/Sunset/Magic Hour

(Circle One)

Characters involved:

_____

Scene opens with:

_____

_____

Basic Action:

_____

_____

_____

What of the characters is revealed in the scene?

_____

What does the scene advance about the story?

_____

What causes your character to take action?

_____

_____

Notes:

_____

_____

_____

_____

## CONSIDER THE FOLLOWING SCENE SUGGESTION:

On the next page, write a scene where the characters who have taught your hero characters also demonstrate they have changed and are better for the experience.

Scene Location Description: Interior/Exterior:

Day/Night/Sunrise/Sunset/Magic Hour

(Circle One)

Characters involved:

Scene opens with:

Basic Action:

What of the characters is revealed in the scene?

What does the scene advance about the story?

What causes your character to take action?

Notes:

## CONSIDER THE FOLLOWING SCENE SUGGESTION:

On the next page, write a scene where a character affected by the actions of the hero explains a moral they have learned.

Scene Location Description: Interior/Exterior:

_____

Day/Night/Sunrise/Sunset/Magic Hour

(Circle One)

Characters involved:

_____

Scene opens with:

_____

_____

Basic Action:

_____

_____

_____

What of the characters is revealed in the scene?

_____

What does the scene advance about the story?

_____

What causes your character to take action?

_____

_____

Notes:

_____

_____

_____

_____

## CONSIDER THE FOLLOWING SCENE SUGGESTION:

On the next page, write a scene where the opponent character admits to the reality the heroes have created through their effort. Develop the characters you have considered the opposition. Do they wane in their resolve?

---

---

---

---

---

EXPERT TIP: Look at your script and arc of your timeline and determine where you can add a few scenes to your story, even if they are extremely short, so long as your story is more rich for the addition. Consider using the scene and character cards, which are available from www.cinema–libre.com, and ask for them at your school store.

Scene Location Description: Interior/Exterior:

_____

Day/Night/Sunrise/Sunset/Magic Hour

(Circle One)

Characters involved:

_____

Scene opens with:

_____

_____

Basic Action:

_____

_____

_____

What of the characters is revealed in the scene?

_____

What does the scene advance about the story?

_____

What causes your character to take action?

_____

_____

Notes:

_____

_____

_____

_____

# Looking for more ideas?
# CONSIDER PARTICIPATING IN THE CINEMA–LIBRE FILM MOVEMENT AND SUPPORT THE CINEMA–LIBRE FILM FESTIVAL

1) To the Cinema-Libre Filmmaker, money does not exist. Cinema-Libre is an expression of pure creativity, free of fears of profitability and commerciality. All filmmakers and films working under the Cinema-Libre Code should recognize the divine state of being and that state's innate ability to create everything from nothing. In this creator's image, all skills, materials, talent, lighting elements, design elements, production equipment and other tools must be native to the artists, borrowed from friends or liberated. Manual labor and other working as a bartering tool is strongly encouraged as the Cinema-Libre Filmmaker is expected to be of service.

2) All films created under the Cinema-Libre Code must be as positive as possible in nature, with the heroes representing loving-kindness and the beauty, truth, and difficulty natural to the state of the human condition. They should further teach tested and real techniques to the audience for the liberation from worldly suffering, as best understood by the filmmakers, including: meditation, presence, communion, forgiveness, sobriety, surrender, self-actualization and finding inner peace, calm, and joy.

3) All Cinema-Libre Filmmakers should, whenever possible, use the tenets expressed by Cinéma-Vérité Filmmakers, combining both ideals to create the Cinema of Truth and Freedom.

# More information is available at www.cinema–libre.org

Made in the USA
Charleston, SC
04 February 2014